Hans Kaldenbach

Act Normal!

99 tips
for dealing with the Dutch

with illustrations by Dragan Strišković

Translated from the Dutch by J.G. Knecht
and Mike Wilkinson

2008 Prometheus Amsterdam

with thanks to:

Chams Berragiy, Karina Boom, Yaron Kaldenbach, Aydin Killi, Adalet Yilmaz Kumçu, Thom Langerak, Helga Ravier, Orsine Resida, Gitta Verhoeven and Selahattin Zorlu.

First impression 1995
Eighth impression (revised) 2006
Tenth impression 2008

Original title *Doe maar gewoon*

English translation Uitgeverij Prometheus, J.G. Knecht and Mike Wilkinson
Author photograph AD/Harry Verkuylen
Illustrations Dragan Strišković
www.uitgeverijprometheus.nl
ISBN 978 90 446 0820 5

Introduction

Do you have contact with the Dutch in your daily life?
If you do, it is important to be familiar with some of their customs. Some of them may seem strange and inappropriate to you, but this is probably due to differences between Dutch culture and your own. Remember, the Dutch may sometimes think *your* culture is strange and inappropriate too.
Here are tips for dealing with Dutch men and women*. They are primarily intended for first generation people coming from Turkey, Morocco, Surinam, the Antilles, Aruba, the Arab world, Africa and Asia.

Are you Dutch?
Take a good look in the mirror, then. Enjoy it – and be ready to be astonished and surprised: this is how other people see you!

Readers from the provinces of Limburg and Brabant say the title should be 'Dealing with Hollanders' (people from the provinces of North and South Holland).
When you have lived in the Netherlands a bit longer, you will understand why.

---

* 'The Dutch' means 'white' Dutch men and women, throughout. You probably read it that way automatically, even though there was no reason to. And by the way, the masculine grammatical form will be used from here on where both sexes are implied: it makes it easier to read.

1
A firm handshake

Many Dutch people may think your handshake is weak. They hate a limp handshake. "Slimy and horrid," they think, immediately getting the impression that you have no 'character'. They automatically start thinking you're a subservient and subordinate type of person. They probably also reckon that you are not very independent and unable to stand up for yourself.
You may notice that a Dutch handshake seems intimidating and domineering. As if they are trying to show you who's the boss straight away. That's not how the Dutch see it. To them, a firm handshake is perfectly normal.
The ten characteristics of the firm Dutch handshake:

(1) You walk up to the other person with your arm nearly fully extended in front of you, and you smile.
(2) When you shake hands, your elbow remains bent, however – not with a straight arm.
(3) You have to use your right hand. If it is in a sling, for example, you have to apologize for not being able to shake hands.
(4) Your hand should be vertical, otherwise they will think you are domineering or subservient.
(5) You then have to push firmly so that the crook of your thumb meets the crook of the other person's thumb.
(6) Now you have to squeeze the other person's hand firmly. How firmly? In an *inburgeringscursus* (naturalization training course) it usually takes about three weeks before people are doing it 'properly'.
(7) Then you shake the hand firmly once, vertically. A couple of small shakes follow naturally. Holding on longer than that is definitely wrong.
(8) Look the other person in the eye while shaking hands.
(9) You need to have a relaxed smile when you do so.
(10) What is also very important is that your thumb presses firmly into the soft flesh above the other person's thumb. It's like the full stop at the end of the sentence: the other person can then tell that you really mean it!

The Dutch do not realise that their handshakes have these ten characteristics. They think that they 'just simply shake hands'.

2
Formal and informal forms of address

Many Dutch adults find it impertinent if you address them with 'jij', the informal 'you' form. Only friends and acquaintances say 'jij' to each other. In the beginning, the best policy is to use 'u', the formal form of address, with all adults (anyone older than 25 or so). After you've known each other for a while, they will suggest switching to the informal 'jij'.
Most Dutch people will be offended if you use the informal 'jij' too soon. It is always the more important of the two (the older one, the boss) who takes the initiative and says that the other can say 'jij'.

3
Keeping their distance

When talking to you, the Dutch maintain a greater distance than you are accustomed to. If *you* keep the normal distance that people from Turkey or Morocco or Surinam are used to, the Dutch will find this intrusive.
If a Dutch conversation partner takes a step back, it means he is uncomfortable. He feels that you are standing too close.
If a Dutch woman feels that you are standing too close, she may interpret this as implying sexual interest.
Dutch people do not touch each other while having a conversation. If you do touch them, you will notice that they are uncomfortable about it: they will think you are homosexual or that you don't know how to behave properly.

4
Being on time

Dutch people often keep track of the exact time. And they are generally punctual. If *you* are late, this will irritate them a lot. The Dutch see not being on time as a sign of being untrustworthy. Someone you can't rely on – not someone a Dutchman

will want to do business with. A person who is late for a job interview will not be hired.
The Dutch don't know a lot about 'foreigners'. But they do know that foreigners are frequently late, which annoys them. "Here I am, on time, and Hassan still isn't here," they might say.
If you want to get on in the Netherlands, you have to learn to be punctual!

Tips:

- *Always be on time. In the Netherlands, it is better to be ten minutes early than five minutes late.*
- *For example, if you have to start work at eight o'clock, then you actually need to be there ten minutes* earlier. *Strolling in at eight means you're too late! Those ten minutes are for taking off your coat, making a cup of coffee, and so forth.*
- *If you make an appointment with a Dutch person, write it down in your diary. The Dutchman can then feel confident that you will turn up as agreed.*
- *If you cannot come, give as much advance notice as possible. The Dutch like to know about a cancelled appointment several days in advance if possible.*

5
Letting the other finish speaking

In the Netherlands, it is considered good manners to let the other person finish what he is saying. In some countries, all talking at once shows you are listening and responding. The Dutch consider it polite to wait until the other person is finished. Then the other speaker gets a turn. This is particularly true of Dutch people from the higher social classes. A Dutchman who has been interrupted might say "Let me finish talking, please" or "You interrupted me". The other person's reaction will usually be to apologize and allow the speaker to finish.

6
'Yes' means 'yes': it's a commitment

If you ask a Dutchman something and he says 'yes', then he's made an agreement. You, might say 'yes' simply to be polite, or just to show that you heard him. Or you might have been trying to avoid an argument or a discussion or friction.
To the Dutchman, 'yes' is a commitment to something. The Dutch find it hugely irritating that many foreigners say 'yes' without actually having agreed to anything. They will consider you to be unreliable.

"Ali, can you come tomorrow at nine o'clock?"
"Yes."
"All right, agreed."
As far as the Dutchman is concerned, a definite agreement has been made!

7

Verbal and nonverbal communication

The Dutch pay most of their attention to your actual words. They don't hear the intonation that you use when saying something. If you casually mention that something will happen tomorrow, they think it really will happen. If you mumble a half-hearted "Yes" in response to something a Dutchman suggests, he thinks you have agreed to it. He won't have noticed your nonverbal "I'd rather not". The Dutch don't understand your reluctance to spoil the atmosphere with a blunt "No" – they've learned to disregard nonverbal signals. They listen to *what* you say, not *how* you say it.

Many Hollanders (i.e. from the west of the country) do not realise that there is a similar habit in the east of the Netherlands. People there may say, for example, *"Ik zal er us aan denken"* (I'll think about it) or *"Dat moeten we maar us doen"* (We really ought to do that); the extra word *"us"* means that *nothing* is going to happen.

8

Dropping by unannounced

The Dutch almost never visit each other without making an appointment first, even with close friends. Even a mother will phone her daughter to find out when it's convenient to come by. People almost never drop by unannounced. The same rules apply to family: first you ring them up ("Would it be OK if we come round today?"). If your visit would not be convenient, they will simply tell you so: "No, today isn't a good day. Come another time if you like." The Dutch don't consider this rude or blunt, just 'honest' and 'straightforward'. In these situations, being straightforward is considered more important than being tactful.

Dutch people will also want to know exactly when you intend to arrive. That gives them time to tidy up the room, send the children to bed and have a steaming cup of coffee ready when you ring the doorbell.

If you do turn up unexpectedly or if you are too early, the Dutch will often say, "Sorry about the mess", even if the house is actually quite tidy. They're actually saying that they could have made the place even cleaner.

9

Taking flowers with you

In Holland, visitors frequently take a bouquet of flowers when they visit. These are given to the hostess, who will usually say, "Oh, you shouldn't have!" Although it sounds ungrateful at face value, it is their way of expressing appreciation. Your bouquet will be placed in a vase at some point during the visit, usually by the lady of the house. She may ask, "Do you mind if I put them in a vase later? Then I can come and join you straight away." "Yes, of course," you reply.

It is particularly important to take flowers if you don't know the people very well: this is almost guaranteed to make a good impression. In recent years, the custom of bringing a bottle of wine as a gift has also become popular. The bottle has to be wrapped up nicely, even though everyone can see at once exactly what it is.

10

You won't automatically be asked to stay for dinner

If you visit a Dutch family at around five thirty p.m., the chances are you will not be asked to join them for dinner. Your Dutch hosts will find it quite normal to begin eating (at six o'clock) without you and they may become rather uneasy because they don't understand why you aren't leaving. If a Dutchman says: "We're going to eat", that's not an invitation to eat with them: he's asking you to go away.
Is that inhospitable? Not to the Dutch. Only very good friends or family members stay for dinner.
As a Dutchman, you would never pay someone a visit after four in the afternoon. Most Dutch households will not be ready to have visitors until after eight in the evening. They may want to watch the news, or maybe they haven't done the washing up yet.
Dutch people are sometimes a bit ashamed of their perceived lack of hospitability, but they can't do anything about it. It's just the way they are.

A considerate Dutch host:
"It's six o'clock. We're going to eat now. Would you like a cup of coffee, perhaps?"

11

Not everything revolves around food

You will discover that Dutch cuisine is not terribly varied and that food does not occupy a prominent place in Dutch life. The attitude is more about 'eating to live' than 'living to eat'. The Dutch also think it is strange to spend a lot of time preparing a meal.
The Dutch say "What we eat doesn't really matter as long as there's plenty of it" – and they really mean that a bit. In the rural areas in the past, you would be asked, "Have you had enough?" It didn't matter whether it was nice or not.

12
Enjoying yourself seems to be a sin

Many Dutch seem to find it difficult to enjoy themselves – it is as if they consider having fun to be a sin. They seem to have an internal barrier that prevents them from enjoying things to the full or letting themselves go. This is evident in their uninspired eating habits, inconspicuous clothing, sober architecture, restrained manner of celebrating and so on. Calvinism (a religious doctrine) has played a considerable role in Dutch history. The Dutch themselves say that Calvinism is to blame for their inhibitions regarding enjoyment, having fun, and expressing their emotions.

13
Act normal!

In Holland, exhibiting material wealth is frowned upon. It is often difficult to judge who's rich and who's poor by the clothes people wear. Expensive cars and jewellery can quickly be considered vulgar. To many Dutch men and women, it is a virtue to just to be normal and blend in with the crowd. People who want to be the best, reach the top or excel in some way do not talk about it in public. These ambitions are almost something to feel ashamed of.
A very frequently used expression is: "Act normal – that's quite strange enough!" One of the things that they appreciated the former queen Juliana for was that she was so 'normal'. Having an 'employee of the month' at work is something that many people find a rather laughable idea.

14

Who pays in a cafe or restaurant?

When the Dutch go out to eat together, it is quite usual to 'go Dutch': everyone pays for their own food and drink. The Dutch do not consider this peculiar. To them, it is simply 'fair'. If you are paying for your own food and drink, you can feel free to order something expensive because nobody else has to help foot the bill. Of course, frugality also plays a part – a reluctance to help pay for other people's expensive tastes.
In a bar, people are expected to take turns to buy a round of drinks. Most Dutch will carefully keep track of who has already bought a round and who has not.

15

Annoyance if you speak your native tongue

Dutch people will find it extremely annoying and inappropriate if you converse with others in your native tongue in their presence. It can make them suspicious: they may think you are talking about *them.* You would probably like to carry on speaking your own language in such a situation, because you feel more comfortable with it. What should you do?

- If you're talking to several compatriots, one of you can speak Dutch to the Dutchman. Or
- One of you can say, "Excuse us. We'd like to talk in our own language for a moment." In most cases, the Dutchman will not feel he's being excluded then.

16

Family ties are less important in the Netherlands

To many Dutch, family ties are becoming less important. Grandparents, aunts and uncles no longer play an important role in their lives. It's the direct family that has priority, not the extended family. There is also a growing tendency to regard friends and acquaintances as more important than family.

A Dutchman might say, "Just because you have a brother or sister doesn't mean you have a good relationship with them." The Dutch probably do not inquire about your family very often either. They don't ask each other about their families either, men least of all. Friends often do not know the simple things about each other's families: whether the parents are still living, how brothers and sisters are doing, and so on. The Dutch see nothing unusual in their parents moving to an old people's home. Most parents would not want to live with their children; they think their children are entitled to lead their own lives. Families with a handicapped child sometimes place the child in a special home. The Dutch consider this a good and humane solution: their child is in good hands. The choice is in no way motivated by lack of compassion or humanity.

17

Everything in life is carefully planned

The Dutch lead very planned lives, although that can be difficult to arrange if both partners are working outside the home.
At ten-thirty a.m., housewives often drink coffee with the neighbours.
Lunch (usually sandwiches) is around one p.m.
At about three p.m. they drink coffee or tea.
Most people eat their hot evening meal at six p.m.
At eight in the evening, they watch the news.
At about eleven, most Dutch people go to bed.
Rituals concerning life's emotional events are also carefully planned and orchestrated.
Funerals follow a standard scenario, with the length of each part precisely planned in advance. The same is also true of weddings and other festivities. This makes the Dutch feel comfortable: nothing unexpected can happen.

18
The weather

The Dutch spend a lot of time talking about the weather. Many conversations begin with it. "Nice weather, isn't it?" or "Who would have thought it? It just won't clear up, will it?" If you want to strike up a conversation with a stranger, talk about the weather: you can't go wrong.
Many people complain about the weather, but most Dutch wouldn't like to live in another climate.
Why do the Dutch talk about the weather so much? Maybe because it's the one thing they are unable to plan for. In their cosy little world where everything is in order, the weather is the only thing that's unpredictable.

19
Adorable little rogues

The Dutch find it amusing when children make cheeky remarks. They think that's healthy precocity. A child bold enough to make such remarks will be able to make its way in the big wide world. It can defend itself. Cheeky children are also quite popular in TV commercials.

The films often have children who rescue the adults from tricky situations. This kind of behaviour is referred to as 'independent'.
It doesn't mean that children can say anything they want. There are limits, but the children aren't very good at finding out where the boundaries are. Cheeky Dutch children will probably be more irritating to you than to the Dutch.

20

To bed on time and no playing outside after six

To the Dutch, 'bedtime' is an important aspect of raising children. A seven-year-old, for example, may know that he has to go to bed at quarter past seven. And Dutch children go to bed on time, not five minutes late! Dutch parents think this is an important part of bringing their children up. On top of that, they want to keep the evening for themselves – no matter how much they love their children.
Dutch parents also consider it very important that their children do not play outside after six p.m. Only on warm summer evenings may children play outside until nine. The Dutch often refer to parents who allow their children to play outside until late as being antisocial – "Those people don't know how to raise their children properly."
These child-raising values are very firmly instilled in Dutch culture. As a result, they frequently clash with the ideas of immigrants who have a more 'out-of-the-house' culture, who often let their children play outside 'too late'.

What does a Dutchman consider a 'nice' neighbourhood?
One where all the children are indoors after six p.m. and where people only put the garbage out after dark.

21

Sex

Sex is discussed more openly in the Netherlands than in many other countries. The Dutch are also less inhibited about nudity, for example on the beach or in the sauna. After sports, they sometimes shower together naked, although men and women usually have separate shower facilities. Topics such as menstrual problems (headaches, cramps) are frequently discussed quite openly. This openness about sex in the Netherlands has only existed since about 1970. Many Dutch see this as an important advance.

Homosexuality is also becoming increasingly accepted in the Netherlands. Many homosexuals are quite open about it and they can also get married.

These are important and integral aspects of their culture for many Dutch people. They sometimes worry that the arrival of immigrants may reverse this progress and they can get quite heated about it.

It might surprised you learn that despite all this, there is still considerable shame and ignorance in the Netherlands about sexuality.

22

Whistling at women on the street

If you're a foreign woman, you will have noticed that Dutch men do not openly show their appreciation for women in public. In France, Surinam, Turkey and Italy, a man lets a woman know he finds her attractive in several ways: prolonged stares, calling out or whistling.

Dutch men do not do this. Although they do look at women, they don't make it obvious. Dutch males consider it unseemly to whistle and call after women. "You're acting like a builder or a navvy," the Dutch women would reply.

If a Dutch woman were to say to a man, "Are you looking at me?" then he would feel ashamed and would apologize at once. You will probably notice that a Dutch man may find it awkward if he wants to make clear that he finds a woman attractive.

23

Showing that you want sex

The Dutch usually show that they want sex in a fairly indirect way. A young man will almost never say to a girl: "How about it, baby?" To a Dutch woman, that would seem much too direct, too irreverent and thoroughly inappropriate.

A young man who wants to sleep with a girl employs a different tactic: talking to her at great length, but not about sex. Then he invites her to "come to my place for a drink". Or she asks him in for "a cup of coffee". This is a kind of code language. In most cases, the real motive is understood by both. But of course all this beating around the bush does lead to misunderstandings. There has therefore been TV campaign and sex education at schools to explain that a girl might genuinely be offering a cup of coffee, and that she does not want sex at all.

In recent years, women have started taking the initiative more often when it comes to sex. This can often make the men more unsure.

24

Do Dutch women seem unfeminine to you?

Many foreign men and women find that Dutch women do not have a feminine appearance and that their behaviour is not feminine either. In their eyes, Dutch women seem far too masculine: they wear trousers, have a masculine gait and make little effort to be pleasing to men.
Many Dutch women find it silly and overdone to wear nail varnish on a daily basis, to wear perfume, skirts or makeup and to pay too much attention to clothes and so forth in general. A low neckline may often be thought of as rather tarty.
Women in the south of the Netherlands do pay more attention to their clothing and spend more than women in the west of the country.

25

Breasts or buttocks?

In some non-Western countries, heterosexual men are primarily attracted to women's buttocks – the fuller the better. Not so in the Netherlands. In general, the Dutch male is more of a 'breast man' than a 'buttock man'.
Dutch women with large buttocks are usually not happy with their appearance. They certainly will not wear brightly coloured shorts to accentuate their buttocks. They are more likely to wear something like a long jacket to make it less obvious.

26

Relationships: understanding, respect and love

In modern-day Holland, understanding, respect and love are considered vital components of a relationship. People want partners who really listen; they consider mutual understanding and respect for one another's feelings to be important.
A hundred years ago, when the Netherlands was a much poo-

rer country, it was a different story. Back then, demands by one partner on the other were more practical than they are now. In those days, it was important to have a husband who did not drink too much or frequent prostitutes. He had to earn a decent income – put the food on the table. The wife's virtues, on the other hand, were thrift (you didn't want a wife who would squander your hard-earned money) and the ability to raise children and mend clothing. Understanding, respect and love were less important back then.

(27)

How do the Dutch move their bodies?

Compared to many people from Surinam and the Antilles, the Dutch have stiff and angular body movements. The Dutch think their way of moving is normal; moving the entire body rhythmically feels exaggerated to them, even when listening to rhythmic music. Sometimes they feel jealous of others whose body movements are fluid and supple, or they may say that it looks 'primitive' to them.

(28)

"Come in"

When you enter a Dutch home, not everybody will stand up. Sometimes people will stand up to shake your hand, but this is not obligatory. If people remain seated, do not interpret this as rudeness. Neither are you obliged to shake everyone's hand, unless this is your first visit. Your Dutch host will not welcome you formally.

You might find this manner of receiving guests uncivilized and rude, but to the Dutch this is simply a relaxed way of greeting visitors.

"Hi there everybody. I'm not going to go around shaking hands with everyone, it's such a fuss."

29
Coffee

Coffee is an essential part of Dutch life. When the Dutch invite you to their homes, they often promptly serve you a cup of coffee or tea. Is this a hint that you should not stay too long? Quite the contrary: in Holland, a steaming *kopje koffie* is a hearty welcome. Your host or hostess will offer you a cookie with each cup – just one cookie, mind you – after which the lid goes back on the cookie tin. The Dutch see nothing uncongenial whatsoever in this ritual. Usually you will be offered a second cup of coffee, again with one cookie.
If you've had enough coffee, you can simply say so ("No thank you. Maybe later"). Don't lay your spoon across the top of the cup, as you might well do at home. This would not be good manners as far as your Dutch host is concerned.
When two Dutch people have something to discuss, a typical starter might be: "Let's have a cup of coffee, shall we?" The same expression is also used when the beverage is not coffee, but tea.

30
'Gezelligheid'

Along with coffee, another essential ingredient of Dutch society is *gezelligheid*. When people reminisce about times gone by it is usually the *gezelligheid* they miss most of all. Dutch who live abroad and are homesick particularly miss the *gezelligheid* of Holland. It is difficult to pinpoint exactly what *gezelligheid* is. It has to do with feelings of snugness, cosiness, security, serenity, homeliness and relaxation.
Drinking coffee can be *gezellig*. Visiting a friend can be *gezellig*. So can an open fire. A neighbourhood can have a *gezellig* feel to it; a painting depicting a domestic setting can also be *gezellig*. If someone refers to you as *gezellig*, take this as a compliment.
After you have been visiting, saying that it was *gezellig* is a smart move. And you can thank them for being good company as they leave after a visit too: "*Bedankt voor de gezelligheid.*"

31
At the dinner table

Dutch table manners might be different from what you're used to. In the Netherlands, table etiquette is as follows:

- Dutch people mostly eat quickly, even when the food is good. They also often prefer to have the courses in quick succession – less waiting around.
- After the meal you sometimes remain seated at the table to talk ('napraten' or 'natafelen' in Dutch).
- After a meal at someone else's house, Dutch guests will say: "Het heeft me goed gesmaakt" (I enjoyed it) or "Het was heerlijk" (That was excellent).
- It is considered very gracious to offer help in clearing the table. Your offer will probably be declined (also polite!), but the fact that you offered is much appreciated. In the Netherlands it is not considered effeminate for a man to help clear the table.
- Asking the cook how the food was prepared will often make a good impression. "Would you mind telling me the recipe for that?"

32
Television

When you visit Dutch people at home, they normally turn off the TV; this is a sign of good manners. They consider it quite disturbing if the TV is left on while they are visiting someone, even if the sound has been muted: their host seems more interested in the television than in his guests!

A Dutchman:
"I visited some people the other day and it was dreadful. They left the television on the entire time. Can you imagine such a thing?"

33

Give my regards to your wife

When saying goodbye, a Dutch man will often say something like "Give my regards to your wife." This is just to show that he has not forgotten his friend's wife even though she is not there. It has no sexual connotations.
If a Dutchman makes this remark to you, an appropriate response would be "Thank you, I will."

34

Helping a woman into her coat

If you (a man) and your wife visit Dutch friends, your Dutch host might get your wife's coat for her as you prepare to leave. He will hold the coat in such a way that your wife can slip into it with a minimum of effort.
You need not feel offended or uncomfortable when this happens. The Dutchman performing this ritual considers it a very polite gesture. Dutch men find helping a woman into her coat the height of courtesy.

35

Adapting to life in Holland

The Dutch sometimes say that foreigners should adapt to the way of life in Holland. They also think that Dutch people living abroad adapt to *their* host country.
But this is not always the case. Many Dutch in Benidorm (Spain) prefer to eat French fries and have a real Dutch dinner. The Dutch community in Australia has its own radio and television programmes. And in the United States, the many Dutch clubs are packed on *Koninginnedag*, the day on which the Queen's birthday is celebrated.
Do you know why some Dutch people are opposed to European unification? They are afraid the Netherlands will have to adapt too much to other EU countries!

You will probably already have noticed that 'adapting' doesn't always actually mean adapting. It mostly means keeping your head down and staying quiet.

(36) *Dogs and cats*

Many Dutch people have a dog or a cat. Their owners buy expensive pet food for them and shower them with affection. Sometimes a dog is allowed to lick his master's face. Most people do not find that unhygienic; they love their dog. To the Dutch, a dog is not an unclean animal!
Pets are important to many people. They aren't as important as a child, but if a pet dies it is mourned by its owners. If a dog or cat dies, it is often buried or cremated.

The Dutch will sometimes even allow dogs and cats to get onto the bed or up onto the table. This is not considered unhygienic either.
Increasingly often, the death announcements in newspapers

include a dog's paw-print or a cat shape. This shows that the dog or cat is also saying goodbye to the deceased.
Fifty years ago, affection for animals was not as strong in the Netherlands as it is today. In this respect, things have changed considerably since then.

The final sentence in a letter from a Dutch couple:
"Kisses to you from us both and a lick from Hector" (the dog).
This is not meant to be offensive; it expresses affection. It shows that not only people are important in Dutch society, but animals as well.

(37) *Religion*

To many Dutch, religion is not very important. If you ask them if they believe in God, the most important thing to realise is that it doesn't really matter to them whether God exists or not. What the Dutch do find important, though, is living an honest life, taking others into account, being fair, and so on. But to them these qualities are entirely separate from God or religion. Most Dutch do not believe it is God's will when something serious happens. They see it as a chance occurrence that could just as easily not have happened.
Fifty years ago the Dutch were a far more religious people than they are today. Nowadays they often find it old-fashioned.

38

The left hand or the right?

In Holland, people give you things with either hand, right or left. Most Dutch do not even notice the difference. They do not have a special hand for personal hygiene or prayer, or for touching unclean things or preparing food. In daily life, they use both hands for everything. They won't understand why you feel offended if they simply happen to have handed you something with their left hand.

39

Pork or beef?

Most Dutch eat any kind of meat; they don't care if it's pork, chicken, or beef. They do not feel an aversion to pork as Moslems and Jews do. The aversion Hindus have to beef is even stranger to the Dutch.
There are Dutch people who do not eat pork, but that's because they believe it is bad for the complexion. Christianity no longer prescribes what its followers should eat. Until about 1960, Dutch Catholics were not allowed to eat meat on Fridays, but that rule no longer applies.

40

Conversations

The Dutch feel that conversations should proceed calmly. Even when disagreeing with each other, they like to maintain their composure. To the Dutch, the normal way to converse is to stay calm and not use your hands excessively. They find your emotional style of conversing rather trying. They want you to hold your hands still and discuss the pros and cons of the matter calmly and without raising your voice.
To the Dutch, even a moderate display of emotion can be seen as excessive. They are afraid that an argument or fight will ensue, particularly if it is among men.

(41)

Getting straight to the point

When the Dutch want to discuss a difficult topic, the usual approach is to plunge right into it. They hardly even take the time to sit and relax. They do not gradually work up to the difficult subject, but come straight to the point.
To you this probably makes a blunt and tactless impression. In some regions of the Netherlands (Limburg and the Eastern Netherlands) the people are more reticent and begin with small talk (*'koetjes en kalfjes'* – cows and calves, a typical Dutch expression) before introducing the real topic.
A Dutch businessman will often handle the business first before going out to eat together. You are probably more used to doing it the other way around.

(42)
Direct language: contradicting one another

If the Dutch do not agree with something, they sometimes make this known in a very direct way. A pupil can say to his teacher, "Sir, you're wrong" or "Sir, you've made a mistake". This is not considered rude in the Netherlands. In fact, this type of direct confrontation is considered very positive.
Perhaps you find it impertinent, but to the Dutch this type of response is both polite *and* direct.
They often make these critical remarks within earshot of others.

(43)
Telling the truth versus lying

Honesty may very well be the characteristic the Dutch value most in themselves. They want you to 'tell it like it is', even when it's painful, even if the truth is blunt or impertinent, and even if it might be hurtful for others. Dutch people will not appreciate it if you tell a 'white lie' to avoid putting someone in an awkward position. They see that as being dishonest: lying.
If a child has stolen money from a parent's purse, the parents may regard the dishonesty involved as being more important than the actual stealing. In a case like that, all Dutch parents will say, "I'm not so worried about the fact that you took the money, but I really am bothered by you lying about it!" The honesty about it is often more important to the Dutch than the actual stealing.
Close family members such as parents are the ones above all that you are expected to be honest with. You might expect that this is where they might take account of other people's feelings out of respect for them and not say anything hurtful. But the Dutch see that as being dishonest.

44

When do the Dutch not tell the truth?

Though the Dutch think of themselves as always telling the truth, this is not the case. Dutch people 'lie' in the following kinds of situations:

- *What do you think of my new dress? Isn't it pretty?*
  It's a match made in heaven.
- *Do I have bad breath?*
  What do you mean? I don't smell a thing.
- *Is everything all right with you?*
  Couldn't be better. And you?
- *Or is it sex you're after?*
  Not at all. Where did you get that idea?
- *Am I right in thinking you're getting irritated?*
  Of course not – I'm perfectly calm.

45

Arguments and opinions

When you ask the Dutch for their opinion, they start by giving you their opinion, and then follow it up with supporting arguments. For example: "I think it's a very good idea because..." Whereas *you* would probably start with the arguments and *then* give your opinion. This is very confusing to the Dutch. They've asked for your opinion but you're giving them the arguments. Often your conversation partner will switch off and stop listening, because he's soon thinking: "She's beating about the bush" or "He doesn't even *have* an opinion."

Which is the Dutchman?
You ask, "What do you think of viewpoint X?"

a. "On the one hand it seems to me... But on the other hand, it's also true that... Which is why I think..."
b. "I'm against it because I think that..."

46
Why?

Dutch people very often ask "Why is that?" or "Why are you doing that?" That is quite normal in the Netherlands. It should not be interpreted as rudeness or impertinence; usually they are simply curious as to why you want a certain thing or why you are doing a certain thing.
In many cases, questions beginning with 'why' are not a sign of protest. Asking 'why' is treating you as an equal, not cutting you out.
However, the Dutch may see a 'why' question from a foreigner as being rude – you're trying to treat them too much as equals.

47
Asking for a promotion

Many Dutch people ask literally for what they want. If for example an employee wants a promotion, it's quite common to ask for it point blank. In many other cultures, this kind of request would not be appropriate. Instead, you would really throw yourself into your work, which would make it obvious that you want a better position.
If a foreigner in the Netherlands works extra hard, his boss will think, "He's working hard, so he must be happy with his job." Dutch bosses don't understand in such a situation that the foreign worker is looking for a promotion. So you have to make it clear, very politely, that that is what you want.

> *A Dutchman to his boss:*
> *"I'd really quite like to do some different work."*
> *or*
> *"I would like to move up to a better position within the company."*

48

I don't know

You will have noticed that people in the Netherlands do not hesitate to say they do not know something. The Dutch do not consider this cause for embarrassment. In a similar situation, you might be used to pretending that you *do* know. The Dutch do not find it impolite or impertinent if you tell them that you don't know something.

49

Do they always want to stand out in the crowd?

Do you think that Dutch people always want to stand out in the crowd? *They* don't look at it this way.
Most Dutch would actually prefer *not* to draw attention to themselves. But they were taught at a young age that it's important to have an opinion on all sorts of topics.
They are also taught that it's very important to express these opinions openly.
But to you, it seems that they are always trying to get noticed. For many Dutch people, being 'critical' is a kind of honesty. You're only worth knowing if you're prepared to speak up.

50
Arguing and making threats

You will not always realise when a Dutch person is angry with you. They often don't show such emotions openly; they may seem distant, or even icily calm. During arguments, most Dutch people reduce the level of emotions in their gestures and words. A Dutchman is most unlikely to say, "I'm going to kill you" or "Just you watch out: I know where you live." If you say something like that, the Dutchman may take it quite literally. He will feel threatened and expects that you really are going to do something; it wouldn't be surprising if he went to the police. A Dutchman who has lost his cool for a moment might say you can drop dead as far as he is concerned, or he might wish a variety of diseases upon you. Or he might call you '*vriend*'; using the word 'friend' in this way means he is on the verge of exploding.

51
An argument has to be cleared up

After an argument, the Dutch will want to talk it over. They'll want to discuss it:

- *Why did you do that?*
- *What did you think that I meant then?*
- *What were you feeling then? And so on.*

You probably feel that talking about it makes it worse and makes you more ashamed, that it's better not to talk about it so openly.

Many Dutch will want to talk the through argument thoroughly first, and only then will they let bygones be bygones. An argument that has not been cleared up is not really over. They will say that it's not yet '*uit de wereld*' (gone from the world, i.e. over) or that '*de lucht is nog niet geklaard*' (the air hasn't been cleared yet). Normal relations can only be resumed after things have been talked through.

(52)

Mother

Dutch people don't understand why you suddenly get so angry if your mother is insulted. They love their mothers too, but they stay much calmer if something negative is said about their mother. It's not such a raw nerve for them. They never insult someone by saying "Your mother is a whore" and neither they would they ever state "I swear it on my mother's honour" or anything like that.
An expression such as "Your mother should have brought you up better" would be unpleasant but will not have much effect. "Does your mother let you do that at home?" might even be seen as a mild and friendly way of correcting someone.

(53)

Not too enthusiastic

The Dutch are not very profuse in their reactions.
When they're satisfied, they prefer to say they are 'not dissatisfied'.
An enjoyable film will be referred to as 'not bad'.
If they think highly of an idea, they'll say, "Yes, there's something to that."
"How are things at work?" "I can't complain."
"How's your health?" "Oh, it could be worse."
The ancient Greeks had a word for this, saying something by denying the opposite: *litotes*. Most Dutch people won't know what the word means, but they're doing it all day long.

54
Taking the initiative

The Dutch consider it very important that people take initiative themselves instead of waiting around until someone asks them to do whatever it was. The Dutch will really appreciate it if you investigate legislation, seek contacts, become familiar with customs, organizations, and so on.
In their eyes, most foreigners are too passive. This often irritates them.

55
Making jokes about the royal family

The Dutch regularly make jokes about their royal family. But they are less inclined to accept the same thing from you as a foreigner. It's rather like making negative remarks about your own family. Criticisms that you would make yourself are not necessarily acceptable from outsiders. The Dutch say that you must adapt completely, but they won't actually let you do so. You can't make the same jokes about royalty ("Just you leave our royals alone"), you can't complain as much about the weather ("Go back to your own country, then") and you can't criticize the government so much ("As if it's any better where you come from"). In fact, you always have to keep a little bit quieter.
This is something that the Dutch often fail to realize about themselves. They believe that they treat everyone equally.

56
Teasing

Many Dutch enjoy teasing each other. When you tease someone you deliberately have a little dig at his honour. For example, Dutch men are particularly sensitive to the insinuation that they are henpecked. And jokes meant to tease often concern the henpecked husband:

"What a pain in the neck! I haven't got any money on me. Could you lend me some?"
"Oh? Didn't your wife give you enough pocket money this week?"

Usually when the Dutch tease each other they don't mean any harm. Teasing is a sign that a person likes you; it means that a friendship is growing between you. Teasing you doesn't mean someone's cross with you! The Dutch often make a game out of countering each teasing remark with an even better remark of their own.
If you want to belong, then it is very important that you can laugh along with these teasing remarks. If you let it show that you feel insulted ('*op de tenen getrapt*' – your toes have been trodden on) then you will be shut out. You are unable to 'take a joke'. This can be tricky, because a tease can be really quite viciously worded.
However, sometimes even the Dutch don't like to be teased. In the Netherlands, men are more likely to do the teasing than women. Inhabitants of big cities do it more than people in the countryside. It's part of the way you can tell who is at the top of the pecking order and who is at the bottom. So teasing is just fun, but it's competitive too.

Someone walks in.
One of the people already there says, "Uh-oh, look what the cat dragged in."
Everyone else knows at once that the two are friends.

57

Emancipated women

In Holland, women are allowed to do just about everything that men do. Dutch men are proud of that. Women are allowed to go to cafes, choose any profession they want, contradict men in public, have an opinion of their own, and so on.

The Dutch often find it irritating when they see a Moroccan or Turkish woman walking two metres behind her husband. To them this is not only backward, but also degrading to the woman in question.

To some extent, however, equality of the sexes in the Netherlands is an illusion. Emancipation for women didn't really make any headway until after 1970. And precisely because emancipation for women is so new in the Netherlands, the Dutch find it doubly irritating to see their not-so-old ways mirrored in foreigners.

However, in the way Dutch people use the language you can still clearly see that men are subconsciously found to be more important than women. Note the word order, for example: men and women, boys and girls, brothers and sisters, and also (unlike English!) nephews and nieces, uncles and aunts, grandpa and grandma. Fred and Wilma. Just as in your circle of acquaintances, the 'most important' people generally come first.

58

Wives and daughters

The Dutch are proud of their wives and daughters, just like you are, but they express it differently. Girls are allowed to go out alone at night, even with boys they don't know very well. The fear of a daughter losing her virginity before marriage is no longer an issue for Dutch parents.

Dutch men don't think their wives and daughters constantly need the protection of a man. When their children go to a party, parents do feel more concerned for their daughters than their sons, but this has more to do with a fear of sexual assault. This explains why daughters are often fetched and brought home afterwards. The idea of a daughter sleeping with several men before she marries does not concern most Dutch parents any more.

> *"I'd rather my daughter have several sexual partners before she marries. I had to find out all those things after I got married."*

59

A woman boss

In recent years the Dutch have begun to find it increasingly normal to have a woman as a boss. Yet a male boss still has an easier time: his subordinates are more apt to believe what he says and his orders are carried out more promptly. People in Holland who want to be progressive act as if it's perfectly normal to have a woman boss.

Female bosses (and most Dutch men) will regard it as totally unacceptable if you refuse to take orders from a woman.

60

The 'me' and the 'we' cultures

Dutch society is often called a 'me culture'. What does that mean? A few examples:

- *If you ask a Dutchman if he believes in God, he'll stop to think about it. This means that everyone will give a different answer.*
- *Dutch parents teach their children that "it doesn't matter what others think of you. All that counts is what you think of yourself."*
- *If a son in a Dutch family steals, this is not a disgrace to his father and brother. It is only a disgrace to the son, because he is the one who did it. In a 'we culture', the entire family is disgraced if the son steals. In such a society, people sometimes say that the parents are at fault if the son steals. To the Dutch, this is highly unreasonable.*

- *Dutch people do not strike up conversations with strangers at the bus stop. Most people don't say a word in the train either.*
- *In the bus or train, most Dutch look for a seat as far away from others as possible. You hardly see any people sitting together!*
- *In general, the Dutch don't mind being alone for a while. In fact, they even enjoy it: this is the Dutch need of privacy. Dutch people who visit Morocco, for example, feel the need to be alone from time to time. Their Moroccan hosts, on the other hand, want to keep them company all day long. If the Dutchman says he wants to be alone, his Moroccan host will think he isn't enjoying the visit. But this isn't the case; the Dutch simply have a greater need for privacy.*

(61)

"Let the police tell them to stop"

In your former country, everyone could correct other people's children in the street. That's no longer accepted in the Netherlands. The Dutch feel that they shouldn't interfere with somebody else's children. And if someone does that to them, their response will be "My child's upbringing is none of your business." They think that everyone is responsible for their own children, outside the home too.

The Dutch will be furious if you say, "They're doing what on the streets? Let the police tell them to stop." They think that you are responsible for your child's behaviour, outside the home as well. They think you are not taking responsibility.

62

Body contact

In Holland, strangers do their best to avoid touching each other. When they want to sit down or walk past others, they will take care to maintain a small space between their bodies. Women in particular do this, but men do as well.
At a crowded party, people sometimes cannot avoid making body contact. If two people's legs accidentally touch, those involved will draw their legs back and say "Excuse me." In the bus or train, people also do their best to avoid bodily contact. In very crowded situations where people cannot avoid pressing against each other, they will excuse themselves. "Sorry about that. It certainly is full here, isn't it?"
Dutch people who are uncomfortable when someone sits very close to them will deliberately choose a chair instead of the couch when visiting a Moroccan family, for example. This should not be interpreted as arrogance.

63

Dutch friends do not always have time for you

Dutch people who are your friends will not always have time for you. Perhaps you may find this confusing. For example, a Dutch friend might say "I don't have time for you tonight." That doesn't mean he's cross with you. Your friend simply wants to do something else tonight and will have time for you another day.
The Dutch would also rather not be disturbed at certain moments. Someone who's reading the newspaper, for example, will want to finish the article he's reading. Only then will he have time for you.

Do you understand why the Dutch sometimes feel that 'foreigners' make requests in a demanding and pushy manner?

---

(64)
Reluctance to be a nuisance

The Dutch do not want to be a nuisance to anyone. This means refraining from talking too loudly in the waiting room or the train, for example. Neighbours do not want to hear each other, so you have to be careful not to have the TV or radio on too loudly at home. For the same reason, doors must not be slammed, but closed gently. The Dutch also get bothered by strange food odours or smelly armpits.
You will probably think that the Dutch get bothered by some very trivial things.

(65)
Indirect orders and instructions

"Give me the salt." That's how people from Surinam and Turkey ask for the salt during a perfectly normal, *gezellig* meal. Hearing this, a Dutchman will think: "Nobody's going to tell me what to do!" To him this is a rude way of asking. He probably won't say so, but he feels offended.
A Dutchman who wants the salt might say:

- *"Could I have the salt?"*
- *"Would you mind passing me the salt?"*
- *"Pass the salt, please."*

Dutch people often have trouble giving instructions, even when in a position of authority that requires it. An employer will say, for example, "Could you manage to type this out before five?" That's not a request, it's an order. It does have to be done by five o'clock, even though that's not the way it's worded. Someone who has a cleaner in to help around the house will hardly dare to say that the bathroom needs special attention. On the note it will say, for example, "Today, could you please..." But it really is meant as an instruction.
Dutch parents also do not *tell* their children what time they have to be home by: they often try to discuss it with their children until agreement has been reached.

Have you noticed the new Dutch use of the word 'aangeven' (to indicate)?
For example: "I indicated to you that this should be filled in." Dutch people feel that words like 'say' and 'tell' sound too much like an order.

66

"You must help me"

The Dutch are particularly allergic to the word *'moeten'* (must/have to). At the desk or counter, many foreigners say "You must help me." Almost all Dutch people will then think something like, "No I mustn't – who are you to tell me what I must do?" It's even worse if you say "You fill it in." They may still help you perhaps, but the reluctance level will be 80 per cent and rising. Naturally, you don't understand why they are being so unhelpful.
A Turkish employee says to his boss, "I must take next Friday off." Later on, you'll hear the boss saying, "Surely you don't think I actually let him have the day off?"
The word 'must' gives the Dutch an impression that you are forcing them to do something. They like it better if you phrase it in the Dutch way: "Could you help me, please?"
If you haven't got a feeling for the way this affect Dutch people, then the best approach is always to say 'please'; that sounds a lot better.

"You must help me, please."
"I must take next Friday off – please."

67

"Don't be so silly"

A major argument once broke out at a company when a Dutch boss said to a foreign worker, *"Doe niet zo gek, joh"* (which means "don't be so silly", but translates literally as "don't act so crazy"). The worker thought his boss was calling him crazy and a major conflict arose.
This expression is always meant in a kindly way. The Dutch only use it when they like you.

There are quite a few other expressions that may lead to misunderstandings.
Do you know what it means – and how seriously it's meant – when someone says the following to you?

- *"Heb ik soms wat van je aan?" (literally, "am I wearing something of yours?" but actually meaning "What are you staring at?")*
- *"Stel je niet aan, joh!" ("Cut the play-acting")*
- *"Doe niet zo idioot!" ("Don't be such a fool")*
- *"Ben je nou helemaal belazerd?" ("Are you totally out of your mind?")*
- *"Ach, krijg het heen en weer!" ("Up yours!")*

68

Now you're really one of us

There are a number of words and expressions that the Dutch don't expect you to be familiar with. You'll notice the amazement in their eyes if you mention participating in the *'vierdaagse'* (annual four-day walking event), say that your child loves *'apekooien'* (a children's gymnastics game), that you're going to the *'aubade'* (music in the morning on the Queen's Birthday) or that you're learning songs for *'Sint-Maarten'* (there are various traditions for the children at Martinmas).
There are also certain turns of phrase that the Dutch will not

expect from you. Ask how old someone's child is, for example. Whatever the age, remark "What a lovely age." Have you been invited somewhere? Say "What shall I bring to go with the coffee?" Have they asked what you want for your birthday? Say "Oh, don't bring anything – your company is more than enough"

69

What do they talk about?

When two Dutch strangers get talking, they see nothing unusual in asking each other what kind of work they do, or where they live and if they like living there. These are not considered private matters.
Perhaps they will ask you similar questions. They assume that other people also find it normal to inquire about these matters.

In Holland it is not acceptable to ask how much a person earns, even if it's someone you know very well. The Dutch do not ask this question either, although they *are* curious about your bank account and income.

70

How to ask for something nicely?

Dutch people who are asking for something nicely always use a 'descending' intonation. Moreover, they also talk more quietly, as if trying to underline how polite they are being.

– *Would you mind moving out of the way?*
– *Hans, have you got another book for me?*

The descending, submissive and slightly pleading intonation makes the question a genuine request, rather than sounding like an order.
You are likely to make such a request in a louder voice and with a different intonation. The tone begins quite high and may even go up further. This can make your question come across as imperative and demanding. *"Hey, Hans, can I have a book?"* A Dutchman will often hear your intonation as ending with an imperative exclamation mark rather than a question mark. This difference in intonation creates a lot of irritations.

71

Movements and gestures

A Dutchman who is calling you might make a movement with his hand which seems deeply offensive to you, as if you are a dog being chased away.
You are not being treated like a dog. This is a case in which a gesture has a different meaning in two different cultures. A wink, for example, does not usually indicate sexual interest. It may mean "Did you get my joke?" A Dutchman complimenting you on your intelligence (by tapping his finger on the right side of his head) is making a gesture that you think means "You're out of your mind." If a Dutchman wants to tell you you're out of your mind, he'll point to the *middle* of his forehead.

72

How do the Dutch tell each other off?

The Dutch have a strange way of telling each other off. They don't say that something isn't allowed; they ask a question!
A teacher who catches a pupil cheating in a test might say "Are you looking at his answers?" or "What do you think you're doing?" The lifeguard at the pool spotting a boy misbehaving would say, for example, "Hey! Do you think she likes you doing that?" or "Would you mind stopping doing that?" or even "Are you having fun?" A policeman who catches someone stealing will say, for example, "So Sir, did you think you could just take it without paying?" or "What are we up to here, then?" What they mean, of course, is that the behaviour has to stop, but they express this by asking a question. Dutch people understand this perfectly well; they give way and acknowledge they were doing something wrong. After all, the guilty feeling is in itself already an important part of the punishment.
If you listen carefully, the subtext of the question sometimes even sounds apologetic. "I'm sorry, but I really do have to bring you into line here."

73

Looking into each other's eyes

The Dutch find it quite normal to maintain extended eye contact during a conversation. Men also do this when talking to women. To the Dutch this is not considered impolite. Nor does it convey sexual interest. Children are taught to look their parents or teacher in the eye when talking to them. If a shopkeeper avoids looking at a Dutch customer, the customer will think "The shopkeeper doesn't want my business."
If you avoid people's glances in Holland, they may think that you're up to no good or that you have something to hide. A Dutch child who is honest (or wants to create that impression) will look you right in the eye and say (for example): "I didn't do it. Honest." If something has been stolen, the child who refuses to meet the questioner's gaze will automatically be considered guilty.

(74)

Confessing to the crime

If a Dutchman is caught stealing, he will usually admit to the theft. He might say, for example, "OK, you're right, I did take it." He'll lower his head a bit and his voice will drop in pitch too. That's how the Dutch show that they are feeling guilty. It's what they would expect someone who has stolen to do.
A Dutchman who wants to admit that he is guilty of something (in the hope of forgiveness, of course) will always do six things:

1. *He says he is sorry.*
2. *He owns up openly to the mistake. "Sorry, I did it."*
3. *He shows regret and remorse and makes it clear that he feels guilty and ashamed: stumbling over his words, head down.*
4. *He then gives the reasons for the mistake.*
5. *He tries to put things right.*
6. *He promises to mend his ways.*

It is very important in the Netherlands not to minimize your own mistakes or to try to blame others for them. You actually have to shoulder the blame with good grace; it's a kind of 'honour' in the Netherlands.
If you act in this Dutch fashion, others will blame you less for the mistake.

"Sorry – I know I'm late. It's very annoying, but please excuse me. There was a huge traffic jam on the motorway and there was nothing that could be done."
Everyone is obviously already well aware of the fact that you are late, but you still have to say so – to admit it, in other words – even in these sorts of situations.
The Dutch sometimes try to turn it to their own advantage. That's known as the "say-sorry culture".

The Dutch get very angry with people who refuse to own up to a crime they have committed. Police and teachers in particular will get furious if they catch Ahmed red-handed and he refuses to admit to the theft. They do not realise that this is exactly how Ahmed is preserving his honour.
In the Netherlands it is normal for someone in a position of authority to admit that they have made a mistake. This is actually appreciated.

75

First a warning, then the punishment

In the Netherlands, it is quite common not to punish someone the first time he breaks a law, but to let him off with a warning. Even the police often choose not to penalize a criminal for his first theft; they give him a 'warning' instead. This means, "We'll forgive you this first time, but you'll be punished if it happens again." And they mean it! To most Dutch, a warning makes them feel guilty and it is a kind of punishment in itself.

76

Showing remorse: "I won't do it again"

In Holland, when a person steals something, he is expected to feel remorse. A person who feels remorse wishes afterwards that he hadn't done what he did. Remorse also implies a resolve not to do it again in the future. That is why someone who feels remorse says "I'll never do it again." If a person is truly sorry,

his conscience makes him feel guilty for what he did.
True remorse, therefore, does not mean you tarnished the family honour because you were found out. It means that your own conscience is making you feel guilty. Many immigrants seem to feel ashamed in such situations – shame that the theft was found out. The Dutch, however, expect the culprit to feel guilty.

77

Aren't there any social values in the Netherlands?

To foreigners it may sometimes appear that there are no social values in the Netherlands. This is not true, but it may seem that way sometimes.
Foreign children sometimes think they can do whatever they please at school. After all, at school it is all right to contradict the teachers, use the informal form of address ('je' and 'jij') and even throw wads of paper about the classroom.
It is always difficult for foreigners to figure out what the values actually are in a new country. The Dutch cannot tell you what their values are either, because they are usually unwritten rules.

78

Smacking your lips at the table

Do you ever eat at the houses of Dutch friends? They learned as children that it is offensive to smack their lips at the table. To a Dutchman, good manners when eating means *not* making any noise and chewing with the mouth closed. You shouldn't be able to look into a Dutchman's mouth while he's eating.
Do you think they aren't enjoying the food? Not so. It's just that the eating habits they were taught are different from yours. The Dutch refer to their eating habits as 'table manners'. They find it really irritating if you smack your lips or slurp your tea. Drinking must also be done silently.

79
Outings

In the Netherlands it is quite common for employees of a company to go on outings together, for example to a bowling alley or restaurant. Company employees also go out to dinner together when the company has something to celebrate, for example a tenth or twenty-fifth anniversary. It will be much appreciated if you go along, even if you think it's a rather peculiar custom. It will really mean you belong.

80
Are the Dutch unpredictable?

Do you find the Dutch unpredictable? This is probably because you are still unfamiliar with Dutch customs, norms and values. In turn, the Dutch often find foreigners unpredictable. This is because they know too little about you.
Don't jump to the conclusion that the Dutch are unpredictable. Try to find out what their rules are.

You have a computer and all sorts of things are going wrong when you use it. What is your reaction?
– "This machine is unpredictable." Or
– "Something's not right, and I don't know how it works."

81
Dutch history

The Dutch do not know very much about their history. They are not very interested in it. They hardly know who William of Orange was, what the Eighty Years' War was about or why Hugo de Groot had to hide in a bookcase. It's all water under the bridge to them. Their national anthem says that they have German blood running through their veins; they may reckon that's a bit odd, but they sing it just the same without thinking about it much.
The Dutch do not like being reminded about the role they played in slavery, apartheid and repression in Indonesia. They have a positive picture of their country in the past as being very civilized: Holland was once a world power and the Dutch ruled the oceans.

82
Insurance

The Dutch seem to be afraid of the future. Almost every Dutchman has several types of insurance: health insurance, homeowners' insurance, personal liability insurance, fire and theft insurance, pension insurance, even insurance for funeral costs.
They have no choice. If their house burns to the ground, their family won't pay for a new house, even if they have the means to do so. If they lose their income due to injury or illness, help from family members and neighbours will be negligible.
"You should have had insurance," is the standard Dutch response.

(83)

The telephone

When answering the phone, the Dutch response will be something like "Van Dalen speaking". If they are storeowners, they will answer the phone with "Good morning, this is Van Dale's Grocery." The Dutch always begin by telling you their name. If you simply say "Hello" when you pick up the phone, the Dutch will think it rather rude.
If you have an answering machine, the standard type of message in Holland goes like this: "This is the answering machine of Mr/Mrs X. Please leave a message after the beep. State your name and telephone number clearly and I will ring you back as soon as possible."

(84)

Meetings

Perhaps you'll become a member of the workers' council at your company or join the parents' committee at your children's school. In that case, it's handy to know the following.
The Dutch have a very fixed approach to conducting meetings. Here are a number of rules usually adhered to during meetings:

- *Each meeting is begun by agreeing which topics will be discussed. Those topics are referred to as 'agenda items'. The topics themselves and the order in which they will be presented are called 'the agenda'. While a particular item is being presented, the Dutch only discuss things relevant to that item. Only after that subject has been formally concluded will the other topics be dealt with.*
  In your native country you may perhaps be accustomed to a less rigidly structured style of conversation.
- *If you wish to discuss a particular topic, you must mention this to the chairman beforehand. You may raise a minor item for discussion at the beginning of the meeting. Quite often you will be asked to express your concerns or opinion in writing. In other*

words, it is not permitted to raise a new topic (a new agenda item) during the meeting. If you do so, a Dutch chairman (if he's doing his job) will say, "That isn't on our agenda for today. We haven't had an opportunity to prepare for it."

- *The Dutch often begin by stating their own opinion. Only later on, when decisions must be made, do they take other people's ideas into account.*
- *If people at the meeting disagree, it is considered important to reach a 'compromise'. A compromise means that everyone gives in a little; no one gets his way entirely, but everyone is satisfied and the meeting can continue.*

85
Anti-German

Many Dutch are a bit anti-German. When they see a German, they may say (half jokingly) to each other, "I want my bike back." This refers to the fact that some Germans attempted to flee back to Germany as World War II neared its end on bicycles stolen from the Dutch.
Anti-German remarks from you, a foreigner, will be rather confusing to the Dutch.

86
Belgians

Every country has jokes about a particular group of people who are reputed to be particularly stupid. For the Turks, it is the Laz people; in Germany, it's the East Frisians. The Dutch assign this role to the Belgians. The Belgians in turn tell jokes about Dutch stinginess.

A Belgian joke:
"How do you know when a Belgian has been correcting a computer text?"
"Because there's Tipp-Ex all over the screen!"

87

Having or sharing

Many foreigners say that the emphasis in the Netherlands is on *having*, that the Dutch are not inclined to share. If a Dutchman in need of money goes to his well-off brother, the brother will often tell him to go and borrow it from the bank. If a Dutchman has a full pack of cigarettes, it is not acceptable to simply reach over and take one. You have to ask permission first ('*bietsen*'). Even if a Dutchman has plenty of cigarettes, he would find it impertinent if you simply took one.
Dutch friends eating cookies in the train will not offer them to a stranger sitting nearby. Each person eats his own share.

88

Keeping business and private matters separate

In differences of opinion or disputes, the Dutch find it important to make a distinction between business and private matters. If a Dutchman has a sharp disagreement with a colleague during a meeting, he will not think it strange to go and have a drink with that person afterwards.
Their rationale is that you have to make a distinction between business matters (the cause of the argument) and private matters. In other words, you can disagree professionally yet continue to be friends on a personal level. That is how the Dutch like to see it, although they themselves do not always succeed in maintaining this division.
Because the Dutch make this distinction between business and private, their prices will also be fixed. It makes no difference whether you are a good friend or a complete stranger: everyone pays the same.

89

Expressing emotions

The Dutch do not find it easy to express their emotions. Men in particular. Flying into a rage is never really acceptable; weeping is only really OK for a short while after a death or a divorce. They *talk* about their emotions more than they express them. The Dutch will talk about sorrow, disappointments, happiness.

In a conflict situation, the Dutchman must also continue to behave 'correctly'. Both his conscience and his culture prevent him from becoming emotional. As a result, the Dutch remain angry for a long time after a conflict. They haven't let their anger out, so they carry on sulking silently. After a conflict, they will often 'talk things over', but they never give their feelings free rein when doing so.

90

The birthday calendar

Many Dutch have a 'birthday calendar' at home, usually hanging on the inside of the toilet door. Birthdays of family and friends are noted on this calendar. If your name appears on this calendar they think quite highly of you! You should never add your own name to the calendar. The Dutch would find that extremely rude.

On a son or daughter's birthday, the entire family is congratulated (wished 'happy birthday'). Not only the birthday boy or girl. "Congratulations for your sister," you might say. Or "Congratulations on your mother's birthday."

Only the person whose birthday it is gets presents.

91

Sinterklaas

Sinterklaas (the feast of St. Nicholas) is an important time for the Dutch. It is celebrated each year on December 5th. *Sinterklaas* is not really considered by the Dutch to be a Christian festival. Although *Sinterklaas* himself bears a striking resemblance to a bishop, to the Dutch he is simply a wise old man with a beard. All Dutch people (except Jehovah's Witnesses) celebrate *Sinterklaas,* even if they're not religious.
On *Sinterklaas,* Dutch people give presents to each other, often accompanied by a short rhyme. These rhymes often contain playfully worded criticism, aimed indirectly at the person receiving the present. *Zwarte Piet* (Black Peter) is a simple-minded, black-skinned attendant of St. Nicholas who talks pidgin Dutch ("I not can talk good"). Many dark-skinned Dutch people object to this figure because they think he reinforces negative stereotypes about them. The Dutch are not usually particularly interested in hearing this kind of criticism: it's *their* tradition.

92
Christmas and the New Year

In recent years, an increasing number of Dutch people have begun giving gifts on Christmas (December 25th). This is another holiday that has lost its Christian significance for many people. They barely know that Christmas is held to commemorate the birth of Jesus Christ. To them, the Christmas tree is not a symbol of Christianity, but part of the cosy feeling surrounding Christmas.

If you want to make a very Dutch impression, send New Year cards in December. Just about everyone sends these cards in Holland, to family and business contacts alike. The card will bear a message along the lines of "Merry Christmas and a Happy New Year". It is important to keep track of which people send you Christmas cards. You should send them a card as well.

In the week before Christmas, your employer will give you a *kerstpakket* ('Christmas package'). This is always a large neatly-wrapped box. Generally it contains expensive food items and other things that are supposed to seem luxurious. There's no rule that says you have to be given a Christmas package, but everyone expects one. Most Dutch people will then complain about what was in it.

93
Here's to your health!

In the Netherlands, a person's health is very important. You can see this in the way they toast and in the way they tell each other off. When toasting, they say: "Cheers! Here's to your health." But when swearing at each other, the Dutch wish all kinds of terrible diseases on each other: telling someone to get typhoid or cholera and so on is about as rude as you can get. They also call each other *kankerlijer* (literally 'cancer sufferer') or *etterbak* (literally 'full of pus').

In your world, honour probably takes a more prominent place. Your toast is to 'honour'; when you swear at someone, you attack that honour by calling his mother a whore or telling him he's the son of a whore.

94

The wish list

In the weeks before *Sinterklaas* and as their birthdays draw near, children make up a wish list. On the list, they write down what they would like to receive.

When people get married, they often have a wish list (or list of presents). This list will either be available at a particular store or at the home of the parents of the bride or groom. People who want to give the bridal couple a gift refer to the list and choose an item in the price range they have in mind. Then that particular gift gets crossed off the list.

Many Dutch find this procedure lacking in spontaneity too, but the practice is growing in popularity. With a wish list, you never get the same gift from three different people.

95

Unwrapping presents

In the Netherlands, the rules for unwrapping gifts are changing. It used to be obligatory to unwrap everything at once, but when there are a lot of gifts (at a wedding, for example) you simply can't open all of them. In that case, the name of the giver must be written on the gift wrapping. The present is unwrapped later and a thank-you card is sent to its giver.

On their birthdays, however, the Dutch *are* expected to unwrap their gifts. Whether or not they actually like the gift they exclaim, "Oh, how lovely. Thank you very much."

If they already have that particular gift, then it's fairly normal to say, for example. "I already have this book. Did you keep the receipt? Then I can exchange it." That's not being impolite, just 'honest'.

Most Dutch people seem unsure what to do with a gift voucher, for books or CD's for example. Not opening it gives the impression that you don't care, but opening it looks like all you're interested in is finding out exactly how much money the other person has spent on you.

96
Living together

In the last forty years or so, it has become common practice for Dutch couples to live together before marriage. The Dutch feel it's better for people to get to know each other first. And a growing number of parents allow their son or daughter to have a girlfriend or boyfriend sleep over.
Around 1960, premarital sex for women would have been absolutely unthinkable in the Netherlands; it was the worst disgrace parents could be faced with. The daughter was thought to be no better than a whore. Christians referred to living together then as 'living in sin'; others used phrases such as 'shacking up' together. In those days, when a girl had a child out of wedlock, her family would insist that she marry right away. It was a disgrace to the entire family.
These days, more and more brides are already pregnant when they walk down the aisle. In this area, values are changing rapidly in Dutch society.

97
Family celebrations are contracted out

In the Netherlands, weddings and a number of other festivities include a meal for guests. These meals are not prepared by the family. Instead, the Dutch will pay a restaurant to prepare a meal and organize the celebration from start to finish.
If a company throws a large party to celebrate its 25th anniversary, it is not organized by the company employees. Either a catering company will be engaged or they will all go out somewhere together.

(98)
Savings stamps

Many Dutch save stamps. These stamps are given when you purchase ten litres of gasoline or –20 of groceries, for example. They are taken home and stuck in booklets. Handing in 250 stamps may for example get you a cup and saucer for half price. If you hand in €12.50 coupons worth, some stores will give you a voucher for a € 15 train ticket. The Dutch greatly appreciate it if you save stamps or coupons for them. The 'points' found on the wrappings of coffee packets are in particular demand.

(99)
Last but not least: frugality

The Dutch are well aware of their reputation in other countries for frugality. It's best not to rub it in. They themselves often do not know what to think of the frugal Dutch mentality. But they won't mind if you smile a bit at their 'waste not' devices: the cheese slicer, the tiny spatula to scrape out the last of the yogurt or whatever from the carton, or the potato peeler. On the one hand, the Dutch are proud of their thrift: they disapprove of people who throw money around ('*geld over de balk smijten*'). But on the other hand they are ashamed of being thought of as stingy.

A Dutch joke about the Dutch:
"Weet u waarom Nederlandse mannen kreunen als ze klaarkomen?" ("Why do Dutch men groan when they come?")
"Omdat het uit hun eigen zak moet komen" ("Because it has to come from their own zak" – the last word meaning both 'scrotum' and 'pocket').

So it's not only amusing to non-natives, because of the dig at the Dutch reputation for frugality, but to the Dutch as well because it's about sex and there's a play on words to appreciate.

Finally: does anyone have a 100th tip?
Is dealing with the Dutch even more difficult than I have suggested?
Please send any hints to: ACTA Kaldenbach, e-mail acta.kaldenbach@tiscali.nl

I would appreciate it!

Hans Kaldenbach
ACTA Kaldenbach

ACTA Kaldenbach specializes in the following areas:
- intercultural advice
- leadership issues
- management
- training

For intercultural aspects, you can contact us about:
- advice for organizations in intercultural aspects
- providing training courses in intercultural management
- providing training courses in intercultural cooperation
- providing training courses in intercultural education
- "train the trainer" workshops
- courses on career advancement for non-native employees
- writing text for publications about intercultural aspects

About the author

Hans Kaldenbach is a consultant/trainer with ACTA Kaldenbach in Zeist and with Centrum Archimedes, the contract work department of the Archimedes Teacher Training Course for the Hogeschool Utrecht (Utrecht College). Hans Kaldenbach provides consultancy and training course in the fields of management and intercultural matters. The following publications are also by Hans Kaldenbach:

- *Diskriminatie, hoe reageer je er op?*
  (Discrimination: how do you respond?)
- *Ik heb niks tegen Nederlanders,*
  101 feiten en insichten uit de multiculturele samenleving
  (I've not got a problem with the Dutch:
  101 facts and insights from the multicultural society)
- *Cultuurverschillen op de werkplek,*
  111 ervaringen met intercultureel management
  (Cultural differences in the workplace:
  111 experiences from intercultural management)
- *Kleur in de klas,*
  101 kernpunten van intercultureel onderwijs
  (Colour in the classroom:
  101 key points for intercultural education)
- *Het lijkt wel of ze geen gevoel hebben,*
  99 tips voor het omgaan met mannen
  (They're just so insensitive:
  99 tips for dealing with men)
- *Waarom makkelijk leven als het moeilijk kan,*
  99 tips om ongelukkig te worden
  (Why take it easy when you can do it the hard way?
  99 tips for making yourself unhappy)
- *Respect! 99 tips voor het omgaan met jongeren in de straatcultuur*
  (Respect! 99 tips for dealing with youth and the street culture)
- *De A is van Amalia, die is allochtoon*

e-mail: acta.kaldenbach@tiscali.nl

This book was originally published as "*Doe maar gewoon*" in Dutch by the same publishers and has also appeared in German as "*Ganz Normal*" and in Arabic.